# Your Wish, Your Command

## P.C. Webber

Publication brought to you by CDL Consulting Group LLC

Your Wish, Your Command
Published by CDL Consulting Group LLC

Copyright © 2022
Written by P.C. Webber, founder & owner of CDL Consulting Group LLC
All rights reserved

ISBN 979-8-218-01420-9

**Admin@cdlowner.com**
**www.cdlowner.com**
**Follow on Instagram, TikTok & Facebook @CDLowner**

No part of this publication may be reproduced, stored in a retrieval system or transmitted in any form or by any means, electronic, mechanical, photocopying, recording, scanning or otherwise, except as permitted under code 107 or 108 of the 1976 United States Copyright Act, without the prior written permission of the author.
Library of Congress Control Number data is available.

Printed in the United States of America

by Hill Print Solutions Dallas, Texas

Original author: P.C. Webber

Original cover design:
Graphics_beach via Fiverr

Editing & layout: *www.absolutepublishingservices.com*

*Disclaimer: This book is based solely based on the author's experiences without guarantees of any sort. Although the information enclosed may be very helpful, individual results may vary.*

## You are appreciated & I love you….

*Jesus for keeping me humble & safe along this journey. Thank you*

*P.C. (I) for putting in the hard work & countless hours just to provide for your children. I truly appreciate your ambition & big heart you have for others. For being loyal to me, thank you.*

*Mama for always pushing me to surpass any small expectation I may have set for myself. You believed in me when I felt like I couldn't see tomorrow. My drive comes directly from you. You never gave up on me when I bumped my head. Thank you.*

*Dad for showing me how to be always a man. Your prayers over the years are appreciated in ways words can't explain. You take my calls during the good, bad, & ugly. For all the times you've reminded me that I can & will do anything I set my mind out on Thank you.*

*Grandma for always putting everyone else's needs before your own. I can count on a gift of some sort from you every holiday. From a little boy taking me to church, to as a man, you've instilled that we need the word of God. Your weekly calls mean the world to me. Thank you.*

Brooklyn for being my motivation for the past 13 years. Raising you has been incredible. Your vibrant smile & goofy personality always makes me happy after a long day. Daughter, I love you first born, my little WNBA player. Thank you.

Cam-Bam for being my motivation for the past 12 years, always being helpful. You are very smart & you've troubleshot your old man with rather simple problems. I love your artistic personality & know you will grow into someone who can put others in position as a leader.

Taco for being my motivation for the past 5 years. You are very outspoken at times & you keep me laughing. Every minute with you is precious to me. Very independent & respectful, I'm proud to be your dad. Thank you.

Family & friends for your support over the years no matter what. Thank you.

*P.C. Webber*

First, I want to thank God for my continued success. Secondly, thank you for you purchase & support.

Congratulations on making your first steps to becoming your own boss. I decided to put this information on paper to serve as a blueprint/how to guide. This book is solely based upon my experiences & individual results may vary. After only 2 years of CDL driving as an employee, I decided to employ myself. They say things don't happen overnight, but change came FAST once I took serious action. My quality of life shifted in ways I could not fathom until this point. Please don't let this guide collect dust after you've read it one time. TAKE ACTION IMMEDIATELY. Thank you again for your support.

*P.C. Webber*

# Owner Operator Training Guide
# Table of contents

**Chapter 1:** About Me & Why ...................1

**Chapter 2:** How to Get Your CDL FREE...................5

**Chapter 3:** W.T.L.F.T.G.M...................9

**Chapter 4:** GameTime...................13

**Chapter 5:** Truck & Insurance & NEVER "Lease Purchase"...................19

**Chapter 6:** IFTA, Fuel Cards, Fleet Team, Day Cab vs Sleeper...................23

**Chapter 7:** Day 1 (My First Day in Business) & OTR vs Local, Relationships...................37

**Chapter 8:** Day 180 & Safety...................41

**Chapter 9:** Negotiate Rates, Contract Work, & IRS Taxes...................45

**Chapter 10:** Day 365...................49

**Chapter 11:** Critical Trucking Terms...................55

# Chapter 1:

### A Little About Me & Why

My name is Phillip. I'm 34 years old. I'm a father of three, single father of my oldest two. Since I was a child, I knew I wanted to be my own boss, especially after getting fired multiple times. I've been a Realtor since 2015. In my first year selling homes, I made over 100K for the first time ever. I was at the closing table twice a month. Life was great! The years following, my sales declined. I eventually burnt out. Ultimately, driving around the city showing homes became taxing. Unrealistic buyers wasting your time. If I don't close this month, my family will starve. For me, it was do or die. Something must change, not now, but right now. Around the time I was trying to figure life out, my family was gone. Things weren't the same. I couldn't provide the life they deserved. Me & my oldest two moved into an apartment across town. That put the battery in my back. NOTHING will stop me. This training is solely based on my experiences. I do not know it all, but I know enough to save you time, money, & stress. When you made this decision to become an owner, you have made a commitment to yourself. Nothing is in the way but you.

Utilize every resource around you, not excuse. I formed my company Brooklyn Cameron LLC (named after my oldest two before my third arrived) in 2017. With no idea what business I was going into, just knew something had to give. I'll be the first to tell you, congratulations driver.

### Why did I choose trucking?

One day at the part time shoe store job I had to get, I thought about freedom. What could give me the time & money I desired? Well, my best friend drove trucks, perhaps I could try that. I had been driving for Lyft & Uber also, I enjoy driving.

My whole life I heard about guys who had successful trucking companies with their own drivers etc. I made my mind up. I want to get my CDL then buy a truck. After failing my pre-trip test 5 times, I got my CDL in 2018. I **worked to learn** for two years. I was screwed on pay by several companies. I knew how to drive, the only thing I wasn't doing was booking the load & receiving all the money. (Well, most, minus the broker's & factoring fees.) One night I wrote my plan down, then immediately acted. That same week, I contacted my nearest **Texas Workforce Commission** office after someone had told me about it. I asked the lady on the other end of the phone about training provided by the state called **WIOA (Workforce Innovation and Opportunity Act)**.

A few days later I came into the office to determine my eligibility based almost entirely on my income, at the time which was about 9 dollars an hour part time. Next, I was scheduled for an orientation regarding the program & the vast opportunities that is provided. Keep in mind, you don't have to go to CDL school. For example, you can get trained to be a certified Electrician instead among many other professions that require some type of license, not a degree.

Please pass this information along as it was a blessing that someone told me about this program as well. I had absolutely no idea about it.

## Chapter 2:

### How did you get your CDL for FREE or other ways?

I got my CDL via the WIOA Program provided by the state of Texas. This program provides funding for training in different types of fields. It is income based & funding is limited. I had to wait about 4-6 months to be approved for CDL training because of funding availability. This method was 100% free to me. Call your local work force commission & ask them if they have programs available that will provide this training.

Program may be called something different outside of Texas* You can also set up payment plans with some CDL driving schools.

You do not have to attend a school to get a CDL. The tuition is $5,000 for school training. There more than likely are qualified private individuals that offer the training in your area, usually about 1500-2500 dollars. *Side note* I recommend training in a 10-speed truck. While the automatics are out there, the 10 speed will be the only some truck companies/owners have. I can drive my 10 speed with my eyes closed. Before I started school, I had never driven a standard (stick shift) car or truck. This entire book is a genuine testament that "If I can do it, you can do it too."

Should you test at DMV in an automatic, your license will say you can only drive automatics on the back. On the flip side, if you train in a 10 speed, there will be no driving restrictions on your CDL.

Another method of obtaining your CDL is renting a truck from a company (accompanied by a valid CDL holder) & train with someone you know. **YOU WILL STILL HAVE TO TAKE WRITTEN & DRIVING TEST AT THE DMV REGARDLESS OF WHICH WAY YOU PURSUE YOUR CDL.** I highly advise going to a school for your training. You will have the opportunity to get extra hands-on time you may need or even hear an answer to a question you haven't thought of yet.

Schools are typically 2-3 months until graduation. *Side note* You don't have to have a perfect driving record. Your license could have been suspended for years, if you clear it up, you will be accepted into most driving schools. My driver's license was suspended for a bit before I enrolled in school. I cleared it up a week before my scheduled start date & kept it moving.

**YOU HAVE TO HAVE A VALID CLASS C LICENSE ON FIRST DAY OF CLASS. THEY WILL KNOW. \*\*ALSO, MANDATORY DRUG TEST ON FIRST DAY/WEEK OF SCHOOL. THIS IS FOR YOUR MEDICAL CARD WHICH**

YOU MUST KEEP IN YOUR WALLET ALONG WITH A VALID CDL. NO FUNNY BUSINESS WHILE TAKING YOUR DRUG TEST, AS THE DOCTOR WILL LITERALLY WATCH YOU URINATE.

ON ANOTHER NOTE:

Get your hazmat, doubles, and triples, plus tanker endorsements ASAP after getting regular CDL.

The hazmat alone sets you apart from many other drivers around you. Transporting hazardous materials is risky, & these companies pay you more money to deliver their loads. It's not always gas, Clorox Bleach is also considered hazardous too for obvious reasons. One of the highest paying loads are REEFER (Temperature controlled loads such as food, flowers, medical items etc.) & Hazmat. (Flammable, explosive etc.). Flatbed work pays very well too.

## Chapter 3:

### Work To Learn First, & Then Get Money.

Why did I choose owner after two years of CDL driving? After the honeymoon phase of being behind the wheel of a semi-truck, I realized I still had no control. No control of where they told me to drive. OTR drivers especially miss key time with family. Out two weeks at a time & home for 2 days by force. You're simply nothing more than a number to the companies that give you an entire spill about why you should come work for them. Just think of how many different companies talked to you in class during your first week of CDL school. Not ONE of them told you how to start a company, and take a chance on you?

I know. I've met several drivers with 25+ years of experience as a company driver. When I ask company drivers why they never became an Owner Operator, they tell me the same thing. "I heard it's expensive", or someone else told them not to do it for whatever reason.

My follow up is usually, "Have you investigated it thoroughly yourself? "

Some people are simply comfortable working for someone else forever. I'm here to tell you, you'll change your life for the better, very fast. I will also say this, I suggest **working to learn first, then get money.** What I mean by that is, go work for a company for at least 2 years. I wasn't fully comfortable driving and backing a semi-truck until 2 years in. Learn how to shift smoothly every time. You should know how to back a 53-foot trailer with minimal pull ups. Ask questions. Take on challenges. I used to pay drivers to back my trailer into the dock. Well one day there was no one around. It was just me & an empty warehouse lot. That forced me to become a professional driver quick. **Work to learn first, then get money.** Don't be in a rush to buy your own truck & start a company. (Especially if you're fresh out of driving school.) Get a job and keep the job as long as you can. Figure out what works for you.

    Within my first year I had loaded & hauled cars & trucks. Strapping tires and making sure the vehicles were secure wasn't my thing. Also driving a 2020 Cadillac Escalade worth over 100K up a ramp was some scary stuff. Imagine doing that while lifting yourself up with a remote. I quit.

    After that, I applied at an end dump company. **End dump** is when the trailer raises to a 180-degree position to release whatever is in it. (Dirt, gravel, metal etc.) I got the job; I was sure I could learn this. Well, there's a technique to dumping. You must drive forward very slowly as it dumps, or you'll roll over. Couldn't conquer that one either.

    On the way back to the yard with my trainer, he asked if I was sure this was for me. Of course, I'm like "yes, I'm sure." (Being optimistic) I was driving down the street & came to a red light that turned green as I approached. I was in neutral getting ready to stop. Suddenly I had to shift back into 6th gear. Well, I missed the shift & made a loud noise. (I scratched the gear.) 10/13 speed drivers know what I'm talking about.

My trainer was PISSED. He cursed at me in Spanish & told me I'm done, which brings me to my next point. **MASTER THE 10 SPEED TRANSMISSION.** It will be rough at first especially if you've never driven a stick shift car like myself. So, my lanes are containers & dry van/reefer trailers. Simple. Within the first two years I was comfortable getting the trailers around corners. I knew how wide to turn. I knew how to shift a 10-speed truck. Oh, another side note drivers, **ALWAYS DO A TUG TEST ON THE TRAILER BEFORE YOU PULL OFF. YOU DON'T WANT TO DROP A TRAILER IN THE LOT.** Like I did.

# Chapter 4:

### Game Time

I started doing research by watching YouTube videos & asking anyone that wasn't in a company truck for advice. From there I determined I wanted Freightliner as my first truck. They are the most universal & economical. Most mechanics can work on them without sending them to a specialty shop. In the next few pages, I will break down the steps needed from A-Z before you complete your first run under your own **authority**.

**Authority** simply means you have met the requirements to be a compliant freight hauler.

Your Company has valid **TXDOT # Texas Department of Transportation *If applicable*, USDOT # United States Department of Transportation, & MC also known as a Motor Carrier Number & met federal insurance requirements along with IFTA.** *If applicable*

I went to several dealers & missed out on awesome deals because of stage fright. After a few months of wasting time, the sales guy that stuck by me sent me one I couldn't resist. My personal credit score was around 530. Several companies told me no, but two told me yes. The terms weren't the best, & the down payment was $12,000. **The total price of the truck was about 33K OUT THE DOOR AROUND 2019.**

If I had took the earlier trucks I looked at, my down payment would have been only $7500, only months earlier. The dealer was nice enough to hold the truck for me for 30 days with $500 down. The clock started ticking the moment I walked out the door. I had promised to bring money every week until I had it paid. I hustled for 30 days straight. After leaving my first couple thousand at the dealership, I knew there was no going back.

Nothing else mattered, only the goal in mind. Come up with this money or lose everything I left there.
I bought my truck from **Arrow Truck Sales 214.951.0122** in Dallas, Texas. My salesperson Mike was extremely patient. Since the writing of this book, Mike has left the company. Still a great place to purchase. If you do happen to stop by, tell them Phill sent you.

**Another finance gem**, one of my students used his **credit card** for his **down payment.** That's one of the benefits of taking care of your personal credit, & he's not even 30 years old yet.

**Things I did before I bought my truck.**

FORMED AN LLC*

The business address of your company should NOT be linked to your HOME. These are public records, the last thing you want is uninvited company. You can do this on the **SOS** website. (Secretary of State)

Filing fee for Texas is about $300. How many times have you spent that on a weekend out or in the mall? Louisiana's filing fee is $105. I highly suggesting hiring an attorney for this part. **YOUR COMPANY NEEDS TO BE FILED PROPERLY.** One wrong click can have you paying more in taxes than you should. **My attorney William Sanders specializes in this field. He can be reached at:**

# williamsanderslaw.com
# Phone: [972] 890 – 8777

His fee is $99 on top of your state's filing fee.

### OPENED A BUSINESS BANK ACCOUNT

I opened my account at my credit union. When you open your business account try a credit union before the huge banks. Credit unions are available to help the community with loans etc. They generally have lower interest rates.

### DUNS NUMBER FROM DUNN & BRADSTREET,

Dunn & Bradstreet is basically Equifax for business credit. Their link is below. They say it take up to 30 days to get it, but I have two. They both came the same day or next FOR FREE! https://www.dnb.com/duns-number/get-a- duns.html **1.800.526.9018**

GET AN **EIN** # (**Employee Identification Number**)

You get this for FREE online from the link below to IRS. You'll instantly get it if your business is properly filed with your state.

https://www.irs.gov/businesses/small-businessesself-employed/apply-for-an-employer-identificationnumber-ein-online

You can also reach them by phone at 1.800.829.4933

ADDED SECOND PHONE LINE TO MY ACCOUNT FOR BUSINESS ONLY

SET UP BUSINESS EMAIL

ORDERED BUSINESS CARDS

GOT LOGO DESIGNED

CONTACTED **THE FEDERAL MOTOR CARRIER ADMINISTRATION (FMCSA)** TO ASK ALL QUESTIONS REGARDINGNEEDS FOR "**AUTHORITY**" (also known as an '**MC' Motor Carrier number**) for $300

OBTAINED **U.S. DOT NUMBER** ALSO FROM FMCSA FOR FREE.

OBTAINED **TXDOT** NUMBER FROM **TEXAS DEPARTMENT OF TRANSPORTATION** for about $350. (Again, Texas is one of the few states that requires its own authority.) Technically I don't need a **MC number** to run **TEXAS ONLY.**

CALLED COMMERCIAL INSURANCE COMPANIES FOR GENERAL QUOTES.

I INTERVIEWED SEVERAL FACTORING COMPANIES.

(You will learn what a factoring company is in a bit).
All of this before I even thought about looking for a truck at a dealer.

### Truck prices??? When I bought my truck.

A semi-truck is the biggest vehicle on the road. They just look expensive right? While that stigma is kind of true, a used semi-truck is very affordable. In 2018 I bought a 2014 Freightliner Cascadia with a double bunk sleeper & working APU unit. It was very clean and had 540K miles. The price OUT THE DOOR was less than $35,000. With my 12K down payment, my remaining balance was low. My monthly payments for my truck were $1,400 a month. Most of you all have financed a Yukon or Charger for more than that. My terms were very short, while interest was very high. It was the price to pay for a finance company taking a chance on me with bad credit & relatively low CDL driving experience. I purchased my truck right before the pandemic hit America. By the time you read this, my same 2014 with 655K miles will easily sell for 70K. Prices are up nationwide for any vehicle. As of May 2022, a 2018 can cost over 100K. Shop, shop, shop.

Look for your truck nationwide. Be sure to have a reliable semi-truck mechanic look over it before you purchase. Do your due diligence, but don't miss out on a good deal *in today's* market by hesitating.

## Chapter 5:

**Truck & Insurance.**

I purchased a 2014 Freightliner Cascadia (10 speed double bunk sleeper) $1,400 a month. I strongly recommend purchasing from a well-known dealer instead of a private individual. The dealer will offer you (in most cases) a free 60–90-day warranty. Then you have the option to purchase the extended warranty. **GET THE WARRANTY.** The private individual won't offer you anything. You can't be cheap in this business. Take care of your truck, and it will take care of you.

Progressive insurance has been my provider since I started over a year ago. My down payment was roughly $3,500. The monthly payment was 2,000 a month. Full coverage, 1 million liability, 100K cargo coverage, 30K trailer interchange coverage (required if you will be pulling trailers for other companies instead of your own.) Since I only did regional work until I went fully local, I only needed coverage for a 500-mile radius. (Saves hundreds) When I started working in the city, I dropped my radius down to 50 miles of home. I also went from a million to 750K liability. (The minimum insurance required by FMCSA) This brought my insurance to $1,600 a month. Keep in mind, I've only had my CDL a little over 3 years. That plays a major role in your payments. I've talked to owners 20+ years of experience of laugh at what I'm paying. One told me he only pays $800 a month. It just it what it is.

SIDE NOTE: You can simply purchase the truck & run under someone's established authority. Now this will not be free. Most carriers charge at least 10% of every load you run under their company authority.

### LEASE PURCHASE: **DON'T DO IT**!!!!!!

A lot of these companies will dress up a lease purchase program with horrific terms. They bait you in with the idea that you'll own a BRAND-NEW truck if you drive for them for whatever period. Think about it. You can't work with any other broker to make money. You ultimately sign up to be a slave to dispatch for that company. I won't mention any names, but you met quite a few during your first week of CDL class. Don't want to go to Colorado Monday? Too bad. Get the load or quit. All those months you spent washing "your baby" will be done. All the payments you made EVERY SINGLE WEEK will mean nothing.

Essentially you helped purchase that truck for them for FREE since you're now the 4th driver that got in and out that same truck this year.

Remember I'm a Realtor as well. To me this is no different from a tenant in a RENTAL PROPERTY. The tenant pays the mortgage and property taxes. Lastly, you didn't get an attorney to define the lease with you.

There are 50 loopholes that protect the company, not the driver/employee. I don't know ONE person who have completed on of those leases. Purchase your truck from dealer or **from private owner after extensive HOMEWORK.**

## Chapter 6:

### IFTA: International Fuel Tax Agreement

**IFTA** is an agreement between the lower 48 states of the United States and the Canadian provinces, to simplify the reporting of fuel use by motor carriers that operate in more than one jurisdiction. Alaska, Hawaii, and the Canadian territories are not required to participate, however all of Canada and Alaska do. An operating carrier with IFTA receives an IFTA license and two decals for each qualifying vehicle it operates. The carrier files a quarterly fuel tax report. This report is used to determine the net tax or refund due and to redistribute taxes from collecting states to states that it is due. Texas does not require an IFTA sticker if you STAY WITHIN THE STATE.

### Day cab/vs sleeper

To make this simple...
A day cab is a semi-truck without the bed. A sleeper is a day cab with the bed. This is made for sleeping after you've run out of hours of service for the day. Both styles will do the exact same thing

power/driving wise. Keep in mind the sleeper has an extra couple foot or so of body making it slightly more difficult to back into a door. Nothing alarming. Sleepers are typically for people that do regional/OTR (Over the road, better known as cross country driving.) Day cabs generally are a little cheaper than sleepers. I chose a sleeper just to be on the safe side. Trying to sleep in a day cab is almost impossible. Hotels can get expensive on the fly if you must spend the night away from home. My suggestion is going for the sleeper.

The day cab is typical for construction job owner operators. (Dumping rocks, dirt, trash etc.) You'll also see the day cab refilling your local gas stations etc. One of my students bought a day cab. I went with him to check it out and test drive it. He wants to stay local; it was a great truck.

## Make: Freightliner Model: Cascadia

## Sleeper

This is 2014 Freightliner Cascadia. I bought this in Dallas, TX around 2019 for only $35,000 with 540K miles. It now has about 655K & is paid for. 10 speed. Very reliable.

**\*THE ONLY DIFFERENCE BETWEEN A DAY CAB IS A BED\***

You won't find this price anywhere currently as of May 2022. I bought my truck right before the pandemic hit & auto prices skyrocketed. Let's just say it's worth a lot more today even with an additional 100K miles added by me.

## Fuel & Maintenance Cards

Apply for Loves Travel Stop credit card. However, Fuelman & Shell are the some of the easiest cards to get approved for via your EIN. Shell gave me 8K with minimal hoops. Filling a semi-truck these days could easily exceed $1000 dollars. Don't pay cash. I used cash for the first 6 months just trying to figure everything out.

Use the credit card, but only responsibly. I would also apply for a maintenance only credit card. ONE brand new semi-truck tire can exceed $500. Things happen on the road; you need to be a ready as you can be.

## Fleet team established

I have at least 4 mechanics I can call for emergency situations. I do routine maintenance at the same 2 places unless I'm too far away from them. Don't get into the habit of taking your investment to different shops because you believe you're saving. It's hard to keep up with the records if you need to have them investigate the database from 5 years ago. I'm not saying you must go to the dealer for the luxury tax all the time. However, for major repairs I would go to the dealer.

They usually offer you a warranty on the work

done at reputable places. You will need a few tire guys for local roadside calls. I found this out the hard way as you'll read in day 1.

**Download these apps to help you find loads** Uber Freight, Convoy, Coyote Go, Freight Power (Schneider), Carrier 360 (J.B. Hunt), Drive XPO.
On those you can bid on loads & book quickly. There are a vast of needs such as **P.O.** (Power Only), **VAN** (Dry Van/ Regular Trailer).

### TRAILER

Try to get a 53-foot **reefer trailer** when you can afford to add to your fleet. You can use one trailer for two needs. You can take a load of fruit at 40 degrees Monday, then Tuesday you can take a load of TVs which obviously don't need to be temp controlled. You'll make more money with your own trailer VS not having one. We're talking about potentially losing 100s of dollars on each load. Remember **REEFER is where it's at.** I have a good friend who drivers liquor across country dedicated and he is, and has been very successful. Next are the most common trailers hauled by an 18- wheeler.

# Reefer Trailer

Trailer for temperature-controlled loads such as frozen meat, fruit, etc.
Also, can transport non-temp controlled loads.

# Tanker Trailer

This trailer is mostly used for transporting fuel to local stations. Almost all tanker loads require the **hazmat endorsement** on CDL. The test wasn't that hard & I highly recommend obtaining it along with the **tanker endorsement.** (Required to haul tanker loads) I suggest taking both tests on the same day.
More than likely you will need both endorsements to haul one load.

# Dry Van Trailer

This trailer can only take non temp controlled loads. (Such as tires, juices, etc.)

# Flat Bed Trailer

Flat trailer for hauling construction equipment, parts, etc. These are most common used for wide loads that require escorts & permits

# Car Hauler Trailer

Self-explanatory, as I mentioned, this wasn't my thing.
**Heavy responsibility**, while still **very rewarding.**

# End Dump Trailer

Most used for construction jobs such as dumping gravel at a site. It also is used to haul scrap metals away etc.

# Container Trailer

These are steel boxes that come from boats across seas. They are imported at ports across the nation & are heavily regulated via United States Customs. These usually contain high value items such as electronics. Some come thru the United States by train. From there, they are loaded onto a chassis & secured at local rail yards for delivery to warehouses for **live unloads.**

*SIDE NOTE* You can do **P.O. (Power Only)** work. This is a fancy term for bring your truck & pick up our trailer.

    I went over two years without my own trailer, it can be done, but as you can imagine PO work can be scarce. Get some type of trailer ASAP

    **BOBTAIL** (Bobtailing): Driving an 18-wheeler with no trailer attached.

## Chapter 7:

### Day 1 (My First Day in Business)

I picked up my truck Friday. Monday, I had my first load booked 2 hours away. I delivered the building supplies then picked up my return load headed back home with my 2nd load.

Unbelievable, I did it. Howard bound! I was just riding along then I heard what sounded like a gunshot. Just like that, a blown tire. My $1400 payout for one day's work was reduced by $550 because of a roadside tire call. That was my first and last roadside emergency to this day. Guess what? **I only had $500 to my name after this was said and done…..which means I had to borrow $50. Kept rolling, never looked** back. Remember HOW BAD DO YOU WANT IT?

### Why I still drive alone.

Simply put, NOBODY will preserve your investment like you. I put in all the work to get this dream off the ground, as you will too. I am in no rush to step down or away, & you shouldn't be either. Learn all you can & have regular work readily available before you bring in the responsibility of an employee. Things can change rapidly in this business.

**Don't hire just anyone.**

When business takes off you will need reliable drivers. Never mix friends in business. I've dealt with people who want something for nothing, As the boss, you're responsible for their pre hire drug screen. You must run background checks on strangers who have applied to your Indeed posting. Many years of experience is key. I hire only 10 years verifiable CDL experience & good driving history.

**OTR/Regional VS Local**

On The Road driving (OTR) typically works for single men or women with minimal responsibility like only having a pet. If you have responsibilities like picking up kids from school daily, local work will be the best for you. I prefer this type of work. There is a myth that says you can't make any money doing local work. That's simply not true. I'll show you some of MY REAL TIME numbers later.

**Broker load boards & apps.**

DAT Load Board & Truckstop Load board have several packages. The most common ones are about

$100 per month. Both apps have data trackers that will let you know what a particular load you're interested in should be paying you. There are several apps that are free that don't require a subscription. Beware these apps will low ball you, but only if you let them. **\*CRITICAL\*** TRY TO BOOK YOUR ENTIRE WEEK OF WORK THE WEEK BEFORE. You don't want to wake up scrambling the load boards and apps looking for a load the same or next day. There will be a slim number of opportunities.

### Relationships/Reputation

I shouldn't have to explain this, but you'd be surprised. Be professional & courteous when you're at these shippers. These shippers and receivers will call these brokers and have you black balled. Your calls will no longer be answered. Emails will stop receiving replies. Problems at these facilities will hurt your business. A simple route that you were a regular on, has now been given to another driver who will take it serious & will not be disruptive for whatever reason. Yes ma'am, no sir. That's it, period.

## Punctuality

Being on time is critical. Stopping to get fuel can easily take 30 minutes. In some cases, it could take up to an hour if there are other trucks in line waiting to fill up. Keep that in mind when you're planning your route. These shippers and receivers have strict timelines.

Staffing at these companies is aligned with the arrival of the trailer. If you're late, now these companies face potential overtime pay for the lumpers/employees.

Most of the time when you deliver, there are other trucks with the same product set around the same time as you to keep things streamline. The person at the window will gladly allow another truck to unload in leu of your presence if you're 5 minutes late. Now that means when you arrive, you'll be waiting for a door to get unloaded instead of just backing in. Furthermore, now you have to call your next load and explain while you will be late for the pickup.

# Chapter 8:

### Day 180

My training wheels came off. I had built enough relationships to keep me busy weekly with the weekends off I desired. Now I'm getting routine calls for extra work they have. Still no repairs needed. I did a few regional runs for decent amounts. By this time, I had locked in with a local company that needed windows delivered to one of your favorite home improvement stores. The rate was $1,000 a day for 6 hours of work. Then one day I took a wrong, which brings us to our next focus point, **safety**.

### Safety

Google and Apple Maps are not reliable for semi-trucks—especially for semi-trucks pulling trailers of any length. I suggest purchasing a brand-new GPS unit specifically for truckers.

Google nor Apple will warn you about how high the bridge that you're approaching is. There are many to choose from, my favorite has been products by Garmin. An ELD better known as an electronic data logger is your best friend especially if you have will hire a driver right off the bat. As you should know, an ELD keeps an eye on the hours of service you have to work, it will let you know when you need to take your 30-minute break during the work day. You will also be alerted about upcoming resets etc. A dash cam that faces the driver and traffic simultaneously is highly recommended. Higher end ones will monitor the speeds ion the trucks. You'll also receive alerts for any hard braking or any other common action that is considered hazardous. I keep a firearm in my truck. As an owner operator you don't have to abide by company rules other than what the shippers/receivers have posted regarding firearms, and of course your local & federal laws. I ride with several firearms, but I also live in Texas & have a license to carry. Truckers drive across America 24 hours/7 days a week.

You've seen trucks parked in the most awkward locations. That driver is tired & passed out in the rear. Please don't play with your life. We all have a family to come home to.

## ROOKIE DRIVING MISTAKE I MADE:

One day I was listening to Google maps. It told me to turn down a county unpaved road to get to my delivery. I took the turn against my better judgement. I had got about half a mile down the road & suddenly my wheels wouldn't go anymore. I kept spinning out in the mud because it had rained heavily that week. I was loaded with valuable materials.

There was nothing I could do to get it out the mud. After several calls to local tow companies, I was forced to leave my truck in the middle of nowhere for over a week. After it dried, I got a company to finally come out. When I met the driver, we discovered my trailer had been broken into & some of the freight was stolen. I had to make call to the broker and tell them not only the delivery wouldn't be on time, but also, we have a bigger problem. Well, that one turn cost me a relationship with a broker that had been good to me for a while. I was paid $-1000-1200 a day for about 6 hours of work. It was all taken away & a claim was filed on my insurance policy. **SO YEAH, GET A TRUCK GPS 911.**

# Chapter 9:

### Negotiate the Rate

These brokers & companies will send you across the nation for $5 if you let them. If you have a **dispatcher**, they should know what they're doing and going to bat for you. A **dispatcher** is a third party that you hire to keep you going so you don't have to waste time finding loads. However, you'll be on the phone with brokers as well. Get the scope of work verbally first.

### TIME IS MONEY!

Doing a local run that has you picking up one day & delivering the next evening isn't good always, unless you pick that night & drop early in AM. It needs to be streamline. The entire job shouldn't take any more than 3-4 hours. The second thing I ask is, "Is the rate negotiable?". They will usually reply "I don't have much in the load, what are you looking to get on this one?" My approach to local work is my truck doesn't move for anything under $450. (50 miles round trip) That's just me.

They will try to be cheap & keep all the money in house from the comfort of their home or reclining chair in an office, meanwhile you'll be doing all the work. If you could get two quick jobs that can be done in under 8 hours even at $400 each, that's 800 a day. That's $4,000 in a 5-day work week, otherwise known as, $16,000 a month, better known as $192,000 every 12 months before expenses & taxes. I don't take regional loads under $750-1000+ each way.

These brokers are trained to win. If the rate is too low, stand on business. DO NOT TAKE IT.

So, the next time they call, & believe me, they will, it's already understood. Now the ball is in your court. On another note, never go out of town without having a return load booked from the same city (or 50 mile or so radius) headed home. Use the data from the paid load board subscriptions to help determine your worth. Rinse & repeat.

**Contract work &/or regular schedule work is key.**

Your first year should be spent **building relationships**. My motto is **WORK TO LEARN FIRST, THEN GET MONEY.** Figure out your niche, whether it's car hauling, or dropping off TVs to Walmart. After your first 50 loads you will have an idea of what works for your business and what doesn't. Once you've done that, you need focus on the specialty, and area of service. Always be sure these brokers know you're always available when they call you. Do favors for brokers. (Extra work etc.) When certain loads come across their desk, they'll think of you. They will only think of you if you've done legit business without any hassles or problems with their loads. Ask your favorite brokers if they have any contract or regular work you can dedicate you truck to. Talk to other owners. Share information. You never know what they can do for you as well. I meet an owner around day 365 who helped me get regular local work that fit my schedule with the children perfectly.

**IRS Taxes**

When the money comes in, don't lose your mind at casinos, car lots, or on airplanes flying across the country 40 times a year. You need to file your business taxes every 3 months. This helps with keeping clean records & plus you don't want a huge tax bill at the end of the year. **YOU WILL BE IN A HIGHER TAX BRACKET.** Suddenly, there are no more tax returns. Time to return those taxes. Hire an accountant/ CPA for these special needs. H & R Block won't cut it for your business needs. I advise setting up a tax savings account. Every time you get a load done, put 10% into that account.

## Chapter 10:

**Day 365**

My truck was paid off within 14 months of my business launch. I did it. This was the best feeling. I had set out on this goal inside of a shoe store with a dream I knew I could turn into reality. It was GOD, hard work, & dedication that got me here. In the beginning of the book, I mentioned I'm a Realtor as well. One day, one of my friends called and said her boyfriend was looking for a place. I helped him with his needs. He mentioned to me that he was an owner operator. (This was while I was in CDL school) Fast forward a year later, he called me and asked if I wanted to do some local work with a local company as they were needing to contract additional owners. This ended up being the best opportunity for me as it is only 4-6 hours of work per day with me back home by noon daily. Let's just say it paid better than ANY local work I've ever done.

**Relationships. I can't stress enough how important that is in any industry.** Stay with me now, here comes the fun part. As I mentioned earlier, I had to borrow $50 for my first day after a blowout. I bought my truck in the middle of the year, so we won't count that.

After my first full year in business, my company exceeded over 200K in business revenue. Did I take it all home? Of course not. Let's give a standing ovation for **EXPENSES!!!** Either way, my life changed for the better, VERY FAST. Lastly, **GET YOUR TWIC CARD 911.** A TWIC card is a Transportation Worker Identification Credential. It is administered after a background check by the Transportation Security Administration (TSA) to those who need unrestricted access to maritime areas, including ports, port facilities, boats, and continental shelf facilities. This is a federal credential that is used by the U.S. Coast Guard and other transportation professionals. This card will make you some GREAT INCOME. Another benefit is that you will have TSA clearance. It expires after 5 years. It cost me $125. Do it ASAP. Contact **IDENTIGO** 844) 321-2124

## Carrier Confirmation for Load

Total Rate: $1200.0

J.B. Hunt Transport, Inc. ("J.B. Hunt"), as a licensed Property Broker, hereby arranges for BROOKLYN CAMERON LLC to transport this load as a licensed Motor Carrier. BROOKLYN CAMERON LLC must call Lindsey Combs for information and ask for load #4D73576.

**Load Details**
56 Miles

**Equipment**
Trailer:
53 DRY VAN
Hazmat: No
Temperature Controlled: No

**Carrier Contact**
BROOKLYN CAMERON LLC
Attention: BROOKLYN CAMERON LLC -

**Requirements**
Driver Load/Unload: Yes
Driver Count: Yes

### Carrier Services

J.B. Hunt offers many carrier services that include: QuickPay, cash advance, direct scanning, and discounts with many reputable vendors. Call your J.B. Hunt representative or visit www.jbhunt.com to learn more about our carrier programs.

### Comments

All appointments must be met. If driver is late, they will either be refused or worked in with no detention paid. On time service is critical on this load!

1. PRELOADED TRAILER IS :LIVE    0

If Shipper and Receiver addresses on the Bill of Lading do not match the tender, your J.B. Hunt representative must be notified!

* Call 800-UNLOAD1 (800-865-6231) to be issued a Comchek number for all Load and Unload services.
* Please have a blank Comchek with you prior to arrival.
* J.B. Hunt will pay all Load and Unload events directly to the Load or Unload service.
* Do not pay out of pocket as you will not be reimbursed for Load or Unload costs.
* Send a copy of the lumper receipt with BOL upon load completion.

51

| Date | Description | | | $ |
|---|---|---|---|---|
| 12/12/21 | | | No | $800.00 |
| 12/10/21 | | | No | $800.00 |
| 12/10/21 | | | No | $800.00 |
| 12/10/21 | | 7. | No | $800.00 |
| 12/10/21 | | | No | $800.00 |
| 12/6/21 | | | No | $750.00 |
| 12/6/21 | | | No | $750.00 |
| 12/3/21 | JB HUNT TRANSPORT INC(35) | | No | $1,200.00 |
| 12/2/21 | JB HUNT TRANSPORT INC(35) | | No | $1,200.00 |
| 12/2/21 | JB HUNT TRANSPORT INC(35) | | No | $1,200.00 |
| 11/30/21 | JB HUNT TRANSPORT INC(35) | | No | $1,200.00 |
| 11/29/21 | JB HUNT TRANSPORT INC(35) | | No | $1,200.00 |
| 11/29/21 | JB HUNT TRANSPORT INC(35) | | No | $1,200.00 |

Remember what I mentioned earlier about **RELATIONSHIPS?**

Well, this is a recent rate confirmation for $1200 for literally 4-6 hours of work. 56 miles of work to be exact. & It was **POWER ONLY.** (I just brought my truck) This was a daily rate M-F with occasional Saturdays. You can do the math. The best part was I was home by noon daily & IT WAS **LOCAL WORK.** That is just one example of the opportunities that come within the multi-billion-dollar business of trucking logistics. Lastly, remember to find what works for you & corner that market. This may take over a year to get familiar on the owner side as I still learn new things daily.

# Chapter 11:

## Key trucking terms

### A

**AFV –** Alternative Fueled Vehicle. A vehicle that runs on something other than gas or diesel.

### B

**Berth –** Sleeping compartment behind the cab.
**BOL:** Bill of Lading. Signed itemized document from shipper/receiver. Basically, your confirmation that the load was picked up or delivered by you, the owner operator.
**Bobtail –** Tractor operating without a trailer.
**Bridge Formula –** A bridge protection formula used by federal and state governments to regulate the amount of weight that can be put on each of a vehicle's axles, and how far apart the axles must be.
**Broker-** Third party that has a contract directly with shipper. This contract basically ensures they will move their freight in a timely fashion at whatever rate they agree to. The broker then turns around and put these loads on the apps and load boards for carriers to call and bid on. The broker almost will never be

transparent with you, the carrier. You won't know exactly how much they are making off each load, which can make it difficult to negotiate effectively. It is common for carriers to use the data provided by load boards to determine a rate. This data included with other carriers have booked this load for in the last 15 days. Don't be cheap when purchasing the load board subscription. **You can take a broker's class and launch under a separate There are other requirements too as brokers are regulated via FMCSA. (Federal Motor Carrier Safety Admin.)**

Bunk – Sleeping compartment behind the cab.

## C

**Car Hauler Trailer:** Can haul 8+ cars/suvs

**Cabover** – Cab-Over-Engine (COE). A type of truck design with the cab over the engine.

**Cargo Weight** – The weight of the loads, gear, and supplies on a vehicle.

**Cartage Company** – A company that provides local pickup and delivery.

**Carrier Packet-** Legally binding docs that have to be signed by the carrier in order to start taking loads for any freight broker.

**CB-** Citizens Band Radio. This is a two-way radio system used to communicate traffic conditions, help requests, and conversation.

**CDL** – Commercial Driver's License. Allows people to drive a truck or bus that weighs more than 26,001 pounds and is used in support of a business. **Chassis Weight** – The empty weight of a vehicle. Also curb weight and tare weight.

**COFC** – Container On Flat Car. Shipping containers on flat railroad cars.

**Common Carrier** – A company that will carry freight for any customer, as opposed to a private or dedicated carrier that only works for one customer.

**Container** – Shipping Container. One giant box, about 20 or 40 feet long that will fit in ships' holds and can also be carried by rail or truck. Some containers are lighter and longer and are only used in rail and road transportation.

**Container Chassis** – A trailer designed to carry containers.

**Contract Carrier** – A company that carries freight for a small number of customers under contract.

**CPM** – Cents per Mile. The per-mile rate at which drivers are paid.

### D

**Deadhead** – A truck & trailer with no cargo, or tractor only (bobtail), traveling over 50 miles to a pickup location.
**Detention-** Money earned for spending more than 1 or two hours on a specific pickup or drop. Details are

ironed out between the broker and CARRIER (another word for the name of the owner op's company name.) during the CARRIER PACKET signing.

**Dispatcher-** Works for the broker. Their job is to keep the carrier's wheels turning with minimal delays.

**Doubles** – A combination of a truck and two trailers.

**Drayage** – Carrying freight a short distance as part of a longer trip. For example, a tractor picking up freight from a rail yard and carrying it 50 miles to its destination.

**Dry Van-** Normal box trailer

**Drop-** Disconnect the trailer at the facility and leave.

E

**EDL** – Electronic Document Interchange. An electronic system for sharing transportation-related documents like bills of lading.

**EOBR** – Electric On-Board Recorder. A device that records information about a truck's trip.

**E-Log** – A computerized system to keep track of their hours of service and miles. The carrier and dispatcher have instant access to this information, which improves their ability to schedule drivers appropriately.

    The federal government favors the use of E-Logs over traditional hand-written logs.

**End Dump Trailer:** Think of a dump truck, but much larger trailer commonly seen at construction sites.

### F

**Factoring Company-** The third party that gets your company paid while they wait to be paid from the broker/shipper.

**Fifth Wheel** – The way tractors and trailers are connected. The fifth wheel accepts a trailer's kingpin and supports the front end the trailer.

**Flatbed** – An open trailer used for carrying construction materials and equipment and other objects of unusual size and shape.

**FMCSA** – Federal Motor Carrier Safety Administration. Regulates the US commercial trucking industry.
**(1.800.832.5660)**

**Forced Dispatch** – When the company dispatcher assigns a load, customer and delivery time to a driver and the driver must take the load or suffer consequences (such as being forced to wait around several hours or another day for another load, or even being fired).

### G

**GAWR** – Gross Axle Weight Rating. The manufacturer's rating of how much weight an axle can carry.

**GCW –** Gross Combination Weight. The total weight of an entire loaded vehicle including truck, trailer, and cargo.

**Governor –** A device that regulates the truck's top speed. Large fleets use these to ensure their drivers stay within guidelines to improve fuel efficiency and safety.

**Grade –** The steepness of a hill. A 5% grade means a hill rises 5 feet per 100. **GVW –** Gross Vehicle Weight. The total weight of a vehicle and everything on it. **GVWR –** Gross Vehicle Weight Rating. How much the manufacturer approves the vehicle to carry.

## H

**Hazmat –** Hazardous materials.

**Headache Rack –** A barrier behind the truck cab designed to protect the driver from behind in the case of a load shifting forward from the trailer.

**Hours-Of-Service –** FMCSA safety regulations governing how long and when drivers may be on duty and driving.

**Hook-** Connect the trailer at the facility and leave.

## J

**Jackknife –** When the tractor and trailer are at a sharp angle to one another.

**JIT** – Just-In-Time. The art of getting goods to a customer extremely close to the time he needs to sell it. This keeps the seller's costs low by reducing inventory.

## K

**Kingpin (axle)** – An axle's wheels pivot around a kingpin.
**Kingpin (trailer)** – Connects the truck to trailer.

## L

**Landing Gear** – Supports to hold up the front end of a trailer when it is not attached to a tractor.
**LCV** – Long Combination Vehicle. A vehicle longer than a double trailer, like a triple.
**Lessee** – A company or person that pays money to use someone else's property.
**Lessor** – A company or person that owns the property someone else is paying to use.
**Lift Axle** – An extra axle that can be lowered and put into use for a heavier load so that the vehicle can meet federal and local weight standards.
**Live Load-** Shipper loads the trailer at the pick-up facility while you wait,
**Live Unload-** Receiver unloads the trailer at drop off facility while you wait.

**Logbook –** A truck driver's book for recording hours and activities during a 24- hour period.

**Logistics –** The art and science of getting people and materials where they need to be when they need to be there.

**Long-haul –** Driving long distances.

**Lowboy –** A flatbed trailer with a low deck used for carrying taller materials like construction equipment.

**LTL –** Less-Than-Truckload. Carrying less cargo than a full truckload weight for a customer. This includes shipping one package or half of a truckload.

**LTL Carrier –** A company that specializes in combining smaller shipments for multiple customers on one truck.

**Lumper Fee-** Third party that is contracted with the shipper or receiver to load/unload product for you instead of their employees. They come with fees around $500. **Always be aware who's responsible for paying that fee before you book the load.**

## M

**M.C (Motor Carrier Number):** This is otherwise known as **AUTHORITY** You can obtain this by applying via FMCSA's website https://www.fmcsa.dot.gov/

## O

**Owner-Operator** – Trucker who owns or leases and operates his own truck(s).
**OTR** – Over-the-Road. Long-haul trucking, as opposed to local or regional.

**P**

**P&D** – Pickup and delivery.
**Payload** – Cargo weight.
**Pintle Hook** – Used to connect doubles and triples.
**Private Carrier** – A fleet that specializes in carrying goods for its own company.
**PSI** – Pounds Per Square Inch. Used to measure pressure in the tires and air brake system.
**PTDI** – Professional Truck Driver Institute. This organization certifies truck driver training programs. It does not teach CDL classes.

**Q**

**Qualcomm** – A wireless communication system that carriers use to keep in touch with drivers. It's like a combination of GPS, email, and text messaging. The system helps the company keep track of its trucks and it helps drivers know the status of their next load and the weather.

**R**

**Relay** – Two drivers start out in two different origin points several hours apart with loaded trucks. They meet in the middle, exchange cargo, and return to their points of origin.

**Receiver-** Where you drop the product off at (Unloaded)

**Reefer** – Refrigerated trailer that has a cooling unit in the front and insulated walls. It's like driving a giant freezer. These are usually used for perishable food items.

**Rate Confirmation-** Signed payment agreement by broker and owner operator for a specific load.

**Retarder** – Helps the brakes slow down the vehicle. Also Jake brake.

**Road Railer** – A trailer made to travel on both road and rail.

**Runaway Ramp** – Often seen on a steep grade, these are wide, soft areas a truck can pull into to slow down when its brakes lose power.

S

**Shipper-** Where you pick the product up from. (Loaded)

**Shipping Weight** – The weight of a truck not including the liquids like fuel and coolant.

**Sleeper** – A space to sleep behind the truck's cab.

**Sleeper Team** – When two drivers work together so one can sleep while the other one drives, allowing freight to move as fast as possible while staying within federal hours of service regulations.

**Sliding Fifth Wheel** – A fifth wheel that can move back and forth to change weight distribution among axles.

**Straight Truck** – A one-piece truck with the cargo area attached to the chassis, as opposed to a tractor-trailer combination vehicle.

## T

**Team** – When two drivers work together so one can sleep while the other one drives, allowing freight to move as fast as possible while staying within federal hours of service regulations.

**TL** – Truckload. A full trailer-load of freight.

**TL Carrier** – A trucking company that carries a single shipper's freight on one truckload.

**TONU-** Truck Order Not Use—Basically, this is free money from the broker for sending you somewhere you didn't need to be, or something goes wrong with the load upon arrival. This usually pays around $250 for your time.

**Tug Test-** This is a technique that ensures you're properly connected to the trailer. This is done by backing under trailer until you hear the trailer *click*. Ensure both windows are down. Then pull the trailer brake and ease off the clutch. The tractor will do a jumping motion but should not move.

**Tractor** – A truck that is made to pull a trailer.

**Tractor Trailer** – A truck and trailer together.

**Transfer Company** – A firm that specializes in handling cross-border transactions.

## U

**Upper Coupler** – Part of the connection between the tractor and trailer, it carries weight from the trailer, and houses the kingpin, which connects to the fifth wheel of the tractor.

**USDOT (United States Department of Transportation)**

## V

**VIN** – Vehicle Identification Number. The manufacturer gives a unique VIN to every vehicle.

## W

**WIM** – Weigh-In-Motion. A way to measure the weight of a vehicle as it rolls through a station, instead of making it come to a complete stop.

## Y

**Yard Tractor** – A tractor that moves trailers around a warehouse or distribution center.

### Expansion

Do not be in a rush to purchase another truck after you've paid off your first. Put things on cruise control. Evaluate the playing field thoroughly. Purchasing another truck prematurely will take you under fast. We're talking hiring another driver 1,200-1500 a week. Insurance adds on, another $1000, fuel for that truck $2500+ a month, not to mention that shiny new truck payment to go along with it all. Keep calm. You'll know when the time is right. An additional truck is an INSTANT $7,000 business expense increase per month.

*The End*

*I truly hope this guide to success works for you. It is my intent to see you do well and not experience the same things I had to coming into this business. Again, this guide is based solely off my experiences in first 2 years of business. I am not a 40-year expert, but I truly hope you have learned something new. Take it easy on the road drivers. Lambos to the moon, but not before* **YOU WORK TO LEARN FIRST, and THEN GET MONEY.**

**Lastly, I would like to thank my best friend Zoe for the inspiration to get a CDL. Without him, there is no telling where I'd be today.** *God bless, goodnight.*

**P.C. Webber**

www.ingramcontent.com/pod-product-compliance
Lightning Source LLC
Chambersburg PA
CBHW050704160426
43194CB00010B/2000